T0371021

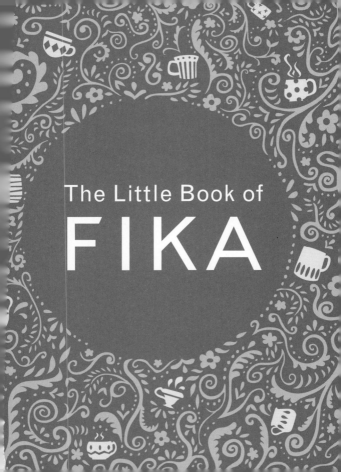

The Little Book of
FIKA

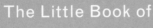

The Little Book of
FIKA

······ ❧ ······

The Uplifting Daily
Ritual of the Swedish
Coffee Break

LYNDA BALSLEV

Andrews McMeel
PUBLISHING®

Swedes are among the world's happiest people

—and for good reason. Yes, their kingdom is admirably egalitarian, progressive, and peaceful, graced with the likes of Alfred Nobel, Astrid Lindgren, and ABBA. Sure, their education is top-notch, their design is exquisite, and they are conscientious stewards of their pristine and vast environment. And certainly, their enviable work-life balance, generous maternity and paternity leaves, and family-friendly society are models for all civilized nations. Clearly the Swedes have much to be happy about, but there's another likely reason for their soaring rates of national contentment: their twice-daily ritual of *fika*.

Fika (fee-ka):

a social coffee break with one's colleagues, friends, date, or family, usually accompanied with sweet baked goods. It can be a noun (let's have fika) or a verb (shall we fika?), describing the act.

Swedes are good at many things, but if there's one thing they do exceptionally well it's enjoy their coffee. Not only do they imbibe the brew, they insist upon at least one if not two coffee breaks a day, which they call *fika*. This ritual is at the core of Swedish culture, and while *fika* literally means "coffee" or "to have coffee" it also represents a happy moment, a time to slow down and focus on simple pleasures— in the form of a coffee, cake, and chat.

In many cultures, the notion of drinking coffee is active and frenetic. A cuppa joe is grabbed on the go, in a take-out cup, meant to be gulped while multitasking. It's considered an energizer, a means to infuse a jolt of caffeine into the system and to rock and roll. Swedish fika is quite the opposite. It's a moment to relax and reflect, connect with friends and family, nature, or oneself. This coffee ritual is at the core of Swedish culture, and it represents a state of contentment that is quintessentially Swedish.

Coffee is a lot more than just a drink; it's something happening. Not as in hip, but like an event, a place to be, but not like a location, but like somewhere within yourself. It gives you time, but not actual hours or minutes, but a chance to be, like be yourself, and have a second cup.

—Gertrude Stein

How did fika begin?

The origin of fika harkens back to the mid-1600s, when coffee was first introduced to Sweden. The Arabic brew arrived in Sweden via trade with Constantinople, the capital of the Ottoman Empire and a long-standing adversary of Western Europe. This was not an auspicious introduction, and coffee's provenance and tendency to perk up the populace prompted Sweden's King Fredrik to deem it subversive and disruptive. Over the next 150 years or so, the king and his successors King Adolf Fredrik and King Gustav III each attempted to deter coffee consumption by either heavily taxing it (which the Swedes refused to pay) or banning it outright, which didn't stop consumption—it simply pushed the coffee movement underground, where it's believed that the word *kaffi* became the colloquial term for the forbidden beverage.

The ban on coffee was finally lifted in 1823, which coincided with the social trend in Sweden to use back slang, or the inversion of syllables in words, so *kaffi* became *fika*. Coffee remained highly taxed in Sweden until 1951, and when the tax shackles were at last removed, coffee forged its caffeine-fueled leap into daily Swedish life. Fast-forward to present-day Sweden, now one of the world's top three coffee consumers, where a day without a cup of coffee is unthinkable and fika is a bona fide social institution.

Today, fika is a necessary component to work-life balance. It's done at home, in cafés (called *fik*), and in the workplace, where there is often a designated time for fika. Stopping and taking a break with your colleagues is not only acceptable—it's expected. It's almost always in the morning and often in the afternoon, as well.

In short, fika is an expression of contentment, finding balance during the day in the pleasure of sipping a cup of coffee. It doesn't get simpler than that.

Science may never come up with a better office communication system than the coffee break.

—Earl Wilson

Did you know?

People who leave their desks two or three times a day to interact with colleagues show a 10 to 15 percent increase in productivity, according to a 2009 MIT study.

Is it really that simple? Yes, thanks to *lagom*.

Lagom is a uniquely Swedish word that does not have a precise English translation. It's directly translated as "around the team," a term that dates back to the Viking era, when mead was passed from person to person, each sipping only their share, and not more, to ensure there was enough for all. It reflected contentment—that there was just the right amount for everyone.

Nowadays, lagom reflects the concept of "not too much, not too little—just enough," a concept of moderation, simplicity, and contentment that has seeped into the Swedish psyche and culture over the ages.

Lagom

(pronounced [ˈlɑːgɔm])
is a Swedish word meaning
"just the right amount."
The archetypical Swedish proverb
"Lagom är bäst"
(the right amount is best),
is also translated as
"enough is as good as a feast."

—Wikipedia

Lagom applies to everything, such as one's general state of being, work-life balance, and personal consumption. It manifests in many ways, including frugality, recycling, clean design, simple food, and, of course, fika. Taking a fika break allows one to find and appreciate balance through the most simple and pleasurable ritual of enjoying a cup of coffee with a small treat, such as a cinnamon bun.

The most simple things can bring the most happiness.

—Izabella Scorupco, Polish-Swedish actress, singer, model

This task of
SIMPLICITY
is perhaps the
most difficult.

Fika 101

Even simple things require practice, so here are
a few essentials to ensure fika success.

Set the time

Give yourself a break during your morning routine.
Leave your desk, step outside, take a walk, go to
a café. Make an appointment to meet your friends.
Catch up on their news and families. Have you
made a new acquaintance or do you want to meet
someone for a first date? Fika is a great way to
break the ice.

Adjust your mindset

Tap into the concept of lagom. Keep it simple and
appreciate the moment. Try not to multitask. Focus
on the ritual of making and pouring the coffee, taking
the first sips of the heady brew. Savor the aroma and
the flavor and indulge in a sweet treat while enjoying
your company or the solitude.

Brew the brew

Coffee is the star of fika, but tea is fine, too—
or even juice or lemonade, if the weather is warm.
The point is the moment, and any beverage that
refreshes is acceptable.

Coffee is a very consuming love . . . it feeds your soul and mind.

Adventure in life is good; consistency in coffee even better.

—Justina Chen, *North of Beautiful*

Did you say "cinnamon bun"?

That's right, fika is all about coffee *and* a sweet treat to go with it—no wonder the Swedes are so happy, right? It could be argued that after soccer, the cinnamon bun is the greatest equalizer in Swedish society. All Swedes, no matter their class or upbringing, have a memory of and love for the cinnamon bun. The mere mention of these sugary swirls of cinnamon goodness transports them back to their childhoods, and no fika would be complete without a soulful cinnamon roll.

The cinnamon bun is the pastry of good thoughts!

—Kaeth Gardestedt, founder of Cinnamon Bun Day, an annual Swedish celebration

Cinnamon buns are so beloved in Sweden, they've been given their own celebratory day, the fourth of October.

Cardamom—
who knew?

After cinnamon, cardamom is the most widely used spice in Swedish pastries, and it's hardly local. Like cinnamon and ginger, cardamom is native to India and was traded on the spice route. The Vikings discovered cardamom on one of their expeditions to Constantinople and returned to the homeland with the spice in their booty.

Did you know?

Sweden is the leading market for cardamom within the European Union.

Lucky 7

Happily, moderation is relative. *Sju Sorters Kako* (*Seven Types of Cakes*) is a popular domestic book from the 1940s, with which every Swede is familiar. Back in the days when housewives baked up a storm, seven was deemed the magic number of cakes to serve for fika. Six cakes were considered too stingy, eight cakes were considered too showy, while seven cakes were—you guessed it—lagom. Today you likely won't encounter seven treats unless it's in a more formal setting, but the concept remains that the amount to be served should be just right (and that number is conveniently open to your own interpretation).

It is the sweet, simple things of life which are the real ones after all.

—Laura Ingalls Wilder

More than just cake

While cinnamon- and cardamom-flecked cakes
and cookies are typical for fika, really any treat is
acceptable. Depending on the time of year, cakes
can be light and fruity, showing off summer berries,
or chocolatey and richly spiced during the winter
season. Precious saffron is a splurge at Christmas,
and ethereal cream-filled buns celebrate Lent
and Easter. Sweet is more common, but savory
is perfectly acceptable, such as artful open-face
sandwiches (*smörgås*) and bread with cheese.

It's the simple things that count

The ritual of fika need not be elaborate, lengthily
planned, or highly organized. You might not be able
to go to a café or have a pre-set time to break from
your work. It can be done simply at home. The key
is to indulge in the ritual and focus on the little

touches. Drape a pretty cloth over a table, choose a fancy plate for serving, use your cherished coffee mug. Pluck a handful of flowers from the garden and arrange the sprigs in a vase as a centerpiece. Light a candle or two in the winter. Set out a few baked sweets for a treat or open that box of chocolates you were saving for a special occasion, nibble a few, and put aside the rest for later. Listen to your favorite music or simply enjoy the peace and quiet.

Will you be out of the house? Pack a thermos, bring a blanket, find a park bench, sit on the beach. It's the intention and practice that make the moment, while the small, thoughtful details make the difference, setting the tone, creating the ambience, and directing your attention to the simple pleasure of fika —no flash required.

Practice makes perfect

The good news is the more you fika, the more engrained it will become in your lifestyle. So, go on, start practicing. Fika is simple, it's delicious, and it's good for you. Tap into your inner Goldilocks and find your balance. Call a friend, put your work aside, walk the dog, or sit in the sun. Savor a steaming cup of coffee and a freshly baked treat. Close your eyes, express gratitude, and experience the moment. And then repeat.

Consider it a caffeinated meditation. You'll find the world will not stop—though you will—and when you step back on the treadmill, you'll feel clear in mind, happy in soul, and sated in belly. You might even feel a little Swedish.

Be content with
what you have;
rejoice in the way
things are. When
you realize there
is nothing lacking,
the whole world
belongs to you.

—Lao Tzu

Happiness is a Swedish sunset— it is there for all, but most of us look the other way and lose it.

—Mark Twain

I like to have

SPACE

to spread my
mind out in.

—Virginia Woolf

I was taken by the power that savoring a simple cup of coffee can have to connect people and create community.

—Howard Schultz

Coffee, the favorite drink of the civilized world.

—Thomas Jefferson

The morning cup of coffee has an exhilaration about it which the cheering influence of the afternoon or evening cup of tea cannot be expected to reproduce.

—Oliver Wendell Holmes Sr.

Coffee
is a
language
in itself.

—Jackie Chan

You have **succeeded** in life when all you really want is only what you really **need.**

—Vernon Howard

All the world is birthday cake, so take a piece, but not too much.

—George Harrison

After Finland and the Netherlands, Swedes are the top consumers of coffee in the world. Swedes drink an average of 18 pounds of coffee per person, per year.

Coffee is the common man's gold, and like gold, it brings to every person the feeling of **luxury and nobility.**

—Sheik Abd-al-Kadir, revered saint of Islam

The present moment
is significant, not as
the bridge between
past and future,
but by reason of its
contents, which can
fill our emptiness
and become ours,
if we are capable
of receiving them.

—Dag Hammarskjöld, Swedish diplomat,
economist, author

Success is getting
what you want;
happiness is wanting
what you get.

—Ingrid Bergman

I adore simple pleasures.
They are the last refuge
of the complex.

—Oscar Wilde

Fika time lasts an average of twenty-four minutes each day for those not working and twelve minutes a day for those at work.

Good communication is as stimulating as **black coffee,** and just as hard to sleep after.

—Anne Lindberg

Coffee refills are free in most Swedish cafés.

He who buys
what he does
not need steals
from himself.

—Swedish proverb

I decide to turn to my old faithful solution to all that is wrong in life. Coffee.

—Lisa Renee Jones, *If I Were You*

Coffee
doesn't ask silly
questions. Coffee
understands.

Sweden allows
up to 480 days
of maternity and
paternity leave for
families. Fathers
on paternity leave
who meet for fika
with their babies in
tow are called
"latte papas."

Life moves pretty fast. If you don't stop and look around once in a while, you could miss it.

—Matthew Broderick as Ferris Bueller
in *Ferris Bueller's Day Off*

Those who wish to sing always find a song.

—Swedish proverb

"Coffee
with a friend"
is really just a
long way to say
"therapy."

The town of Alingsås, in western Sweden, claims to be the fika capital of Sweden, with more than 30 cafés.

Drink your tea slowly and reverently, as if it is the axis on which the world earth revolves—slowly, evenly, without rushing toward the future.

—Thich Nhat Hanh

Nothing is too much trouble if it turns out the way it should.

—Julia Child

Coffee is a hug in a mug.

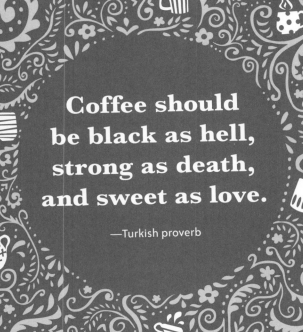

Coffee should
be black as hell,
strong as death,
and sweet as love.

—Turkish proverb

Fika
Recipes

Beverages

French Press Cardamom Coffee

Serves 2

Ever since the first Viking voyagers returned to the homeland with cardamom in their treasure chest, Swedes have had a love affair with the Indian spice. So it's no surprise that they embraced the equally exotic (though Middle Eastern, to be exact) tradition of adding cardamom to their coffee.

Note: This recipe makes 2 servings in a 4-cup (17-ounce) French press. For perfect temperature, warm the press and coffee cups with hot water, then drain before using.

1 ounce whole roasted coffee beans, about
   5 tablespoons ground

4 cardamom pods

1½ cups water

Steamed milk and sugar, for serving

1. If the coffee beans are whole, put them, along with
   the cardamom pods, in a coffee grinder to achieve
   a coarse, even grind and add to the press. (If the
   coffee is pre-ground, grind the cardamom pods
   in a spice grinder, coffee grinder, or mortar with
   pestle and add to the ground beans.)

2. Bring the water to a boil. Pour about ½ cup of the
   water into the press and gently stir. Let stand for
   30 seconds to allow the coffee to bloom.

3. Pour in the remaining water, and place the lid
   on the press, without plunging the filter. Let the
   coffee steep for 4 minutes.

4. Slowly press the filter down. Serve the coffee
   immediately with steamed milk and/or sugar,
   if desired.

Behind every successful woman is a substantial amount of coffee.

—Stephanie Piro, artist

Once you wake up and smell the coffee, it's hard to go back to sleep

—Fran Drescher

Masala Chai

Serves 2

Have no fear, tea lovers, you can fika with
tea, too. Indian-spiced chai (tea) is warm,
milky, and comforting; a perfect beverage
on a chilly day and alternative to coffee.
Medjool dates impart mellow sweetness
while the water steeps. If you prefer sweeter
tea, add honey to taste. Almond milk may
be substituted for cow's milk.

1½ cups water

6 cloves

4 cardamom pods, crushed

2 Medjool dates, pitted

1 (3-inch) cinnamon stick

1 (1-inch) knob of fresh ginger root, peeled and sliced

1 teaspoon black peppercorns

2 cups whole milk

1 tablespoon black tea, such as Assam

Honey, optional

1. Combine the water, cloves, cardamom, dates, cinnamon stick, ginger, and peppercorns in a medium saucepan and bring to a boil over medium-high heat. Lower the heat to medium-low, partially cover the pot, and simmer 10 minutes.

2. Add the milk and tea and simmer 5 minutes.

3. Pour the mixture through a fine-mesh strainer into warm mugs and serve immediately with honey, if desired.

Red Glögg

Serves 6

During the dark winter months, steaming cups of glögg are a cozy way for Swedes to keep warm. Glögg is a rich and heady concoction of mulled wine, fortified with raisins plumped in aquavit (a Scandinavian spirit distilled from potatoes or grain, frequently flavored with caraway) and fragrant with Christmas spices and fruit, such as cinnamon, cloves, raisins, and orange. While a mug of glögg for your morning fika break may not be helpful for work productivity, it is entirely acceptable to imbibe in the afternoon when the winter sun begins its descent. It's especially delicious when accompanied by a ginger cookie.

½ cup dark raisins

¼ cup aquavit

2 unwaxed oranges, preferably organic

¾ cup ruby port wine

½ cup packed light brown sugar

1 cinnamon stick

1 teaspoon whole cloves

½ teaspoon whole black peppercorns

1 (750-ml) bottle medium to heavy-bodied red wine, such as Syrah or Zinfandel

1. Combine the raisins and aquavit in a small bowl. Let stand at room temperature for at least 30 minutes.

2. Peel the skin of the oranges, without the pith, using a vegetable peeler and juice the oranges. Combine the orange peel and juice, the port wine, brown sugar, cinnamon stick, cloves, and peppercorns in a small saucepan. Bring to a boil over medium heat and reduce the liquid by about half.

3. Strain the syrup through a fine-mesh sieve into a large saucepan. Discard the solids. Add the raisins with their soaking liquid and the red wine. Cover the pot and gently warm the glögg over medium-low heat until the wine is hot, without letting the wine come to a boil.

4. Taste for sweetness and add more sugar if desired. Ladle the glögg and raisins into mugs and serve warm.

Coffee with
friends is like
capturing
happiness in
a cup.

White Glögg

Serves 6

White glögg is the brighter, fruitier version of red glögg, with white wine perfumed and flavored with citrus, ginger, and honey. Don't let its golden color deceive you—this glögg is laced with rum and equally potent—a perfect concoction to soften the chill of a dark winter day.

½ cup golden raisins

¼ cup, plus ½ cup dark rum, divided

1 unwaxed lemon, preferably organic

1 unwaxed orange, preferably organic

½ cup granulated sugar

1 (1-inch) knob fresh ginger, sliced

1 cinnamon stick

1 bay leaf

1 teaspoon coriander seeds

½ teaspoon whole black peppercorns

1 (750-ml) bottle medium sweet white wine, such
   as Riesling or Gewürztraminer

¼ cup honey

1. Combine the raisins and the ¼ cup rum in a small
   bowl. Let stand at room temperature for at least
   30 minutes.

2. Peel the skin of the lemon and orange, without
   the pith, using a vegetable peeler, and juice the
   lemon and orange.

3. Combine the peels and juice, the remaining ½ cup rum, the sugar, ginger slices, cinnamon stick, bay leaf, coriander seeds, and peppercorns in a small saucepan. Bring to a boil over medium heat and reduce the liquid by about half.

4. Strain the syrup through a fine-mesh sieve into a large saucepan. Discard the solids. Add the raisins with their soaking liquid, the white wine, and honey. Cover the pot and gently warm the glögg over medium-low heat without letting it come to a boil.

5. Taste for sweetness and add more honey if desired. Ladle the glögg and raisins into mugs and serve warm.

Fear less, hope more; eat less, chew more; whine less, breathe more; talk less, say more; love more, and all good things will be yours.

—Swedish proverb

Elderflower Cordial

Makes about 1 quart

The flavors of Swedish summer are captured in this elderflower syrup. Elderflowers grow prolifically during the Scandinavian summer. The flowers are snipped from the bushes and brined overnight with lemon in a simple syrup, where they impart their delicate floral and honey flavor. Elderflower syrup is commonly added to water as a child-friendly soft drink, stirred into wine and cocktails, or drizzled over fruit or ice cream.

Note: When using fresh elderflowers, use the flower heads only. Trim and discard the leaves and stems, as they contain toxins.

15 fresh elderflower heads, leaves and stalks
trimmed and discarded

2 unwaxed lemons, preferably organic

1 quart water

2¼ cups granulated sugar

1 teaspoon citric acid (sour salt)

1. Soak the elderflower heads in water to
dislodge any dirt or insects. Drain, gently
rinse, and drain again.

2. Peel the skin of the lemons, without the pith, using
a vegetable peeler. Thinly slice one lemon and
juice the remaining lemon.

3. Combine the water and sugar in a large saucepan
over medium heat. Bring to a boil, stirring to
dissolve the sugar. Remove from the heat and
cool to room temperature.

4. Add the lemon peels, lemon slices, lemon juice,
the elderflowers, and citric acid to the syrup. Stir
to thoroughly combine and submerge the flowers.
Cover the pot, and let stand at room temperature
for 24 to 48 hours.

5. Line a fine-mesh sieve with cheesecloth and place over a large bowl. Pour the syrup through and squeeze down on the solids to extract as much juice as possible. Discard the cheesecloth and solids. Pour the syrup into sterilized jars and refrigerate for up to 4 weeks.

6. To serve, mix 1 part elderflower syrup with 3 parts water, white wine, or sparkling wine.

A life without love is like a year without summer.

—Swedish proverb

Cakes & Buns

Cinnamon Rolls
(Kanelbullar)

Makes 24 buns

If there is a single sweet bread that best represents the Swedish sweet tooth, it is the *kanelbullar,* or cinnamon roll. Classic coffee accompaniments, they are ever present at breakfast and, of course, fika. Swedes grow up eating these soft, doughy, cinnamon-swirled rolls, and they are a favorite among young and old alike.

Dough:

1½ cups whole milk

2 (¼-ounce) packages (4½ teaspoons) active
  dry yeast

1 teaspoon plus ½ cup sugar, divided

6 cups unbleached all-purpose flour

2 teaspoons ground cardamom

½ teaspoon sea salt

½ cup (8 tablespoons) unsalted butter,
  melted and cooled

1 large egg

1. To make the dough, heat the milk in a small
   saucepan over medium-low heat until lukewarm
   (110°F). Add the yeast and 1 teaspoon sugar and
   let stand until dissolved.

2. Combine the flour, the remaining ½ cup sugar,
   the cardamom, and salt in the bowl of an electric
   mixer fitted with a dough hook. Add the milk
   mixture, the butter, and egg.

3. Mix on medium-low speed until the dough is smooth and elastic, about 10 minutes. Cover the bowl with a kitchen towel and let rise in a warm draft-free space until doubled in volume, about 1 hour.

4. Divide the dough in half and roll out each half into a rectangle about 9 by 12-inch wide and ¼ inch thick.

Filling:

½ cup (8 tablespoons) unsalted butter, softened

¼ cup granulated sugar

¼ cup packed light brown sugar

2 tablespoons ground cinnamon

1 large egg

2 teaspoons water

Pearl sugar

5. To make the filling, divide and spread the butter over each dough. Whisk the sugar, brown sugar, and cinnamon in a bowl. Divide in half and sprinkle over the butter.

6. Roll up each dough lengthwise, starting with the long side. Using a sharp knife, slice each roll into about 12 (1-inch-thick) pieces. Place the slices, cut side up, on two rimmed baking sheets. Cover each with a kitchen towel and let rise at room temperature for 1 hour.

7. Preheat the oven to 425°F.

8. Whisk the egg and water in a small bowl. Brush the rolls with the egg wash and sprinkle the pearl sugar over the tops.

9. Bake the cinnamon rolls in the oven until golden, 8 to 10 minutes. Cool slightly and serve warm or at room temperature. The buns are best eaten within one day of baking. Once cooled, store in an airtight container at room temperature.

Caradamom Buns
with Almond Cream Filling (*Semlor*)

Makes 12 buns

Originally served exclusively on Shrove
Tuesday, these luscious cream-filled
cardamom buns are now enjoyed
throughout the weeks and days leading
up to and during Lent. *Semlor* (plural for
semla) get a double leavening boost with
yeast and baking powder, which produces
a light and fluffy dough. The buns are
best eaten immediately.

Buns:

1 cup whole milk

1 (¼-ounce) package active dry yeast
(2¼ teaspoons)

1 teaspoon, plus ¼ cup sugar, divided

3 to 3½ cups unbleached all-purpose flour

2 teaspoons baking powder

1 teaspoon ground cardamom

½ teaspoon sea salt

5 tablespoons unsalted butter, melted

1 teaspoon finely grated orange zest

1 egg plus 2 teaspoons half-and-half, for brushing

1. To make the buns, heat the milk in a small
   saucepan over medium-low heat until lukewarm
   (110°F). Add the yeast and 1 teaspoon sugar,
   and let stand until dissolved.

2. Combine 3 cups flour, baking powder, the
   remaining ¼ cup sugar, the cardamom, and salt
   in the bowl of an electric mixer fitted with a
   dough hook.

Add the milk, butter, and orange zest. Mix on medium-low speed until the dough is smooth and elastic, about 10 minutes. The dough should be slightly sticky but not too sticky. If necessary, add more flour, 2 tablespoons at a time, to achieve the desired consistency.

3. Cover the bowl with a towel and let rise in a warm, draft-free space until doubled in volume, about 1 hour.

4. Preheat the oven to 400°F. Line a baking sheet with parchment.

5. Transfer the dough to a lightly floured work surface. Divide the dough into 12 balls. Place on the baking sheet, about 1 inch apart. Let rise 30 minutes. Brush the buns with the egg and half-and-half mixture. Transfer to the oven and bake until golden, about 15 minutes. Remove from the oven and transfer the buns to a rack to cool completely.

Filling:

7 ounces marzipan, coarsely grated

½ cup half-and-half

2 cups heavy cream

2 tablespoons confectioners' sugar, plus more
  for dusting

¼ teaspoon vanilla extract

6. To make the filling, first cut off the top third of
the buns. Using a teaspoon, scoop out the centers,
about ¾ inch deep, without tearing the crust from
the bun bottoms and place the bread pieces in
a bowl. Add the marzipan and half-and-half and
mix to form a sticky mass. Fill the buns with the
mixture.

7. Whip the cream, sugar, and vanilla in the bowl
of an electric mixer until stiff peaks form. Spoon
it over the filling. Place the tops on the buns,
sprinkle with confectioners' sugar, and serve
immediately.

Did you know? There is an anonymous Stockholm blogger who goes by the name Semmelmannen (the Semla Man) who eats one semla each day from February 1 to Shrove Tuesday and reviews in meticulous detail the quality of the bun, cream, almond paste, and appearance.

There's no denying the addictive qualities of semlor: In 1771, Swedish King Adolf Fredrik died after gorging on 14 semlor doused with milk.

A party without cake is just a meeting.

—Julia Child

Saffron Buns
(*Lussebullar*)

Makes 24 buns

These fragrant golden buns are traditionally eaten on Santa Lucia Day, December 13, which pays homage to Lucia, the patron saint of light. At one time December 13 was thought to be the shortest day of the year, and Sweden continues to celebrate this date as the return to lighter days with local communities, churches, and schools organizing processions led by young girls dressed in white gowns and wearing crowns of candles, serving coffee and *lussebullar*.

½ teaspoon saffron threads

11 tablespoons unsalted European-style butter

2 cups whole milk

2 (¼-ounce) packages active dry yeast
  (4½ teaspoons)

1 teaspoon plus ⅔ cup sugar, divided

½ teaspoon sea salt

6 to 7 cups unbleached all-purpose flour

1 large egg, lightly beaten

½ cup raisins, plus extra for garnish

1. In a small mortar or bowl, crush the saffron and a pinch of sugar with a pestle or spoon until finely ground.

2. Melt the butter in a large saucepan over medium-low heat. Add the milk and heat until lukewarm (110°F).

3. Place the yeast in a large bowl and add ¼ cup warm milk and 1 teaspoon sugar. Let stand until the yeast dissolves, 2 to 3 minutes.

4. Add the remaining 1¾ cups milk, the saffron, the remaining ⅔ cup sugar, and the salt. Stir once or twice to blend.

5. Add 6 cups flour to the bowl and stir with a wooden spoon to combine. Stir in ½ cup raisins. The dough should be sticky but not overly wet. If necessary, add a little flour at a time, to achieve the desired consistency. Knead the dough until it pulls away from the bowl and is smooth and elastic, about 8 minutes, sprinkling with extra flour if still too sticky. Cover the bowl with a kitchen towel and place in a warm draft-free spot. Let rise until doubled in volume, about 1 hour. Punch the dough down and let stand at room temperature for an additional 45 minutes.

6. Preheat the oven to 450°F and line a baking tray with parchment paper.

7. Roll the dough into shapes by grabbing a small handful and, with light hands, rolling out into a ½-inch-thick rope. Shape the rope into an S shape or braid two ropes together. Place the

shapes on the baking tray about 1 inch apart.
Repeat with the remaining dough.

8. Lightly brush the breads with the egg and garnish
the folds and corners with a few raisins. Bake
in the oven until puffed and golden, 10 to 12
minutes. Cool slightly on wire racks. Serve warm
with butter. Once cooled, the buns may be stored
in an airtight container at room temperature for
up to 2 days and reheated in a 250°F oven to serve.

Apple Cake
(Äppelkaka)

Serves 8

This cake couldn't be simpler and is a
testament to the Swedish notion that less
is more. It's not overly sweet and is often
served with coffee or for breakfast. Choose
baking apples that are crisp, tart, and sweet,
such as Granny Smith or Braeburn.

1 cup unbleached all-purpose flour

½ cup almond flour (meal)

2 teaspoons ground cinnamon, divided

1 teaspoon baking powder

¼ teaspoon sea salt

¾ cup plus 1 tablespoon granulated sugar, divided

½ cup unsalted butter, softened

2 large eggs

¼ cup whole milk

1 teaspoon vanilla extract

3 Granny Smith or Braeburn apples, peeled
and cored

1. Preheat the oven to 350°F. Butter and line a 9-inch
springform pan with parchment and butter the
parchment.

2. Combine the flour, almond flour, 1 teaspoon
cinnamon, the baking powder, and salt in
a small bowl.

3. In the bowl of an electric mixer fitted with a paddle attachment, cream ¾ cup sugar and the butter until light and fluffy, 2 to 3 minutes. Add the eggs, one at a time, mixing well after each addition.

4. Combine the milk and vanilla in a separate small bowl.

5. Add the flour to the batter in thirds, alternating with the milk and finishing with the flour, mixing to combine after each addition.

6. Cut two apples into ½-inch dice. Add to the batter and mix to combine. Pour the batter into the prepared pan and spread evenly.

7. Slice the last apple, lengthwise, into ½-inch-thick pieces. Toss with the remaining 1 tablespoon sugar and remaining 1 teaspoon cinnamon. Arrange the slices on the top of the cake, gently pressing into the batter.

8. Bake the cake until a tester comes clean, 40 to 45 minutes. Cool slightly and serve warm or at room temperature. Once cooled, the cake may be stored in an airtight container at room temperature for up to 2 days.

You don't have to cook fancy or complicated masterpieces, **JUST GOOD FOOD** from fresh ingredients.

—Julia Child

Sticky Chocolate Cake
(Kladdkaka)

Serves 8

Kladdkaka is very popular in fika cafes, and it's no surprise why: It's essentially an under-baked chocolate cake or brownie with a firm top that cracks open, exposing its gooey center. When the cake is removed from the oven, the center will be runny. Let it cool for at least 1 hour to allow the center to slightly firm up to sticky perfection.

1 cup unbleached all-purpose flour

¼ cup unsweetened cocoa powder

⅛ teaspoon sea salt

2 large eggs

1 cup sugar

½ cup unsalted butter, melted and cooled

2 teaspoons vanilla extract

Confectioners' sugar

Whipped cream and strawberries, for serving

1. Preheat the oven to 350°F. Butter and line a 9-inch round cake pan with parchment and butter the parchment.

2. Combine the flour, cocoa powder, and salt in a small bowl.

3. Whisk the eggs and sugar in a medium bowl until pale and fluffy, about 2 minutes. Fold the dry ingredients into the egg mixture. Add the butter and vanilla and stir until smooth. Pour the batter into the prepared pan.

4. Bake until crisp on top but soft in the center, about 20 minutes. Remove from the oven and cool to room temperature. Once cooled, the cake may be stored in an airtight container at room temperature for up to 3 days. To serve, sprinkle confectioners' sugar over the top. Serve with whipped cream and strawberries, if desired.

You can't buy happiness, but you can buy cake and that's kind of the same thing.

Strawberry Cream Cake
(*Jordgubbstårta*)

Serves 8 to 10

At the height of summer, when the sun and strawberries are at their peak, midsummer festivities prevail on the longest day of the year, replete with feasting, drinking, and bonfires. No midsummer celebration would be complete without a *jordgubbstårta*, with its multiple layers of airy vanilla cake and sun-kissed berries slathered with whipped cream, as a luscious homage to the season. This cake is best eaten immediately. The cake layers may be prepared up to a day in advance, wrapped in plastic and stored at room temperature before assembling.

Cake:

2½ cups unbleached all-purpose flour

2 teaspoons baking powder

½ teaspoon sea salt

4 large eggs

1½ cups granulated sugar

1 cup whole milk

½ cup unsalted butter, melted and cooled

2 teaspoons vanilla extract

1 teaspoon finely grated lemon zest

1. To make the cake, preheat the oven to 350°F.
   Butter and line two 9-inch round cake pans with
   parchment and butter the parchment.

2. Combine the flour, baking powder, and salt in
   a small bowl.

3. Whisk the eggs and sugar in a medium bowl until
   pale and fluffy, about 2 minutes. Whisk in the
   milk, butter, and vanilla. Add the flour mixture
   and lemon zest and mix to combine.

4. Pour the batter into the prepared pans and bake until a tester comes clean, about 25 minutes.

5. Cool the cakes on a rack. With a serrated knife, cut the cakes, horizontally, into two equal layers.

Filling:

3 cups heavy cream

¼ cup sifted confectioners' sugar

½ teaspoon vanilla extract

For Serving

1 pound small strawberries

8 ounces fresh raspberries

6. To make the filling, beat the cream, confectioners' sugar, and vanilla until firm peaks form.

7. To assemble, set aside four to six of the smallest strawberries and six raspberries for decorating the top of the cake. Hull and halve the remaining strawberries (quarter if large).

8. Arrange one cake layer on a serving plate and spoon a layer of cream over the cake. Top with a few of the halved strawberries and the raspberries. Repeat the layering process, finishing with the cream and finally the reserved berries. Serve immediately.

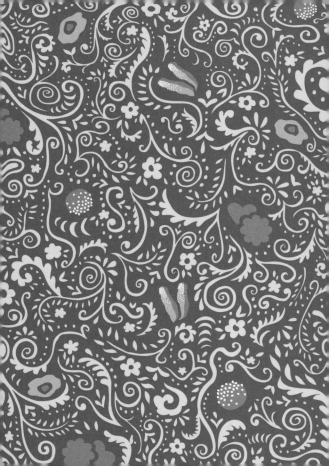

Cookies & Confections

Almond Cookies
(Mandel Kakor)

Makes 20 cookies

Almond is another popular ingredient in Swedish desserts, and these little cookies get a double dose with almond flour and almond extract. They are twice baked, similar to biscotti in method, and gloriously rich with butter. Bake them longer for a crispy cookie or shorter for a tender cookie.

½ cup unsalted butter, softened

½ cup granulated sugar

1 cup unbleached all-purpose flour

½ cup almond flour (meal)

2 teaspoons baking powder

¼ teaspoon sea salt

2 tablespoons heavy cream

2 teaspoons almond extract

1 teaspoon finely grated orange zest

1 egg, lightly beaten

Pearl sugar, optional

1. Preheat the oven to 350°F. Line a baking sheet with parchment.

2. Cream the butter and sugar in the bowl of an electric mixer until light and fluffy, about 3 minutes. Add the flour, almond flour, baking powder, and salt and mix to blend. Add the cream, almond extract, and orange zest, and mix to combine.

3. Form the dough into a ball and divide in half. Roll each half out into a 10-inch log on parchment, and flatten each to about ¾ inch thick. Refrigerate for 15 minutes.

4. Preheat the oven to 350°F.

5. Brush each log with the egg and sprinkle with pearl sugar, if using. Bake in the oven until the logs begin to color and are firm to the touch, 12 to 14 minutes. Remove from the oven and reduce the oven temperature to 300°F.

6. Cut each log crosswise into ¾-inch slices. Return to the oven and bake 12 to 15 minutes for a tender cookie or 18 to 20 minutes for a crispy cookie. The cookies may be stored in an airtight container for up to 4 days.

Seventeen percent of Stockholmers claim to fika at least twice a day.

Swedish Butter Cookies
(Spritzen)

Makes 40 cookies

Simple butter cookies are a Scandinavian classic and a Christmas cookie essential. *Spritzen* are traditionally made with a cookie press, through which the dough is squirted (or spritzed) to make simple or decorative shapes. Do not grease or line the baking sheets. The dough should be pressed directly onto the pan so there is no slippage while baking. You will need a cookie press to make these cookies.

2¼ cups unbleached all-purpose flour, sifted

½ teaspoon sea salt

1 cup unsalted butter, softened

¾ cup granulated sugar

2 large egg yolks

½ teaspoon vanilla extract

½ teaspoon almond extract

Sprinkles for decorating, optional

1. Preheat the oven to 375°F.

2. Whisk the flour and salt in a bowl.

3. In the bowl of an electric mixer fitted with a paddle attachment, cream the butter and sugar until light and fluffy, about 3 minutes. Mix in the egg yolks and the vanilla and almond extracts. Add the flour and mix on low speed until just combined without overmixing.

4. Force the dough through a cookie press fitted with your desired shapes, about 1 inch apart, onto an ungreased baking sheet. Sprinkle with decorations, if using.

5. Bake until light golden, 8 to 10 minutes. Remove from the oven and cool for 5 minutes, then remove the cookies with a spatula and transfer to a wire rack to cool completely. The cookies may be stored in an airtight container for up to 4 days.

Fikabröd

are the freshly baked goods
that accompany coffee.

Ginger Cookies
(Pepparkakor)

Makes about 30

Pepparkakor are available year round but are most popular during the Christmas season, when they're often accompanied by a mug of glögg. Loaded with spices, they are typically served plain, but feel free to decorate with icing if you wish. For crisp cookies, roll the dough out to ⅛-inch thickness, and for chewier cookies, roll the dough out to ¼-inch thickness.

1¾ cups unbleached all-purpose flour

1 teaspoon ground cinnamon

1 teaspoon ground ginger

1 teaspoon ground cardamom

1 teaspoon baking soda

½ teaspoon ground cloves

¼ teaspoon sea salt

½ cup unsalted butter, softened

½ cup granulated sugar

¼ cup dark brown sugar

2 tablespoons unsulfured molasses

1 teaspoon vanilla extract

1 large egg

1. Combine the flour, cinnamon, ginger, cardamom, baking soda, cloves, and salt in a bowl.

2. In the bowl of an electric mixer fitted with a paddle attachment, beat the butter, sugar, brown sugar, molasses, and vanilla until smooth. Add the egg and mix to combine.

3. With the mixer on low speed, gradually add the flour mixture, mixing until just combined. Remove the dough, wrap in plastic, and refrigerate for 2 hours.

4. Preheat the oven to 350°F.

5. Roll out the dough ⅛ to ¼-inch thick on a lightly floured surface. Cut into your desired shapes with cookie cutters. Place on cookie sheets, about 1 inch apart, and bake until firm, about 10 minutes. Remove from the oven and let cool 1 to 2 minutes, then transfer the cookies with a spatula to a rack to cool completely. Collect the remaining dough, roll into a ball and repeat until all the dough is used. The cookies may be stored in an airtight container for up to 1 week.

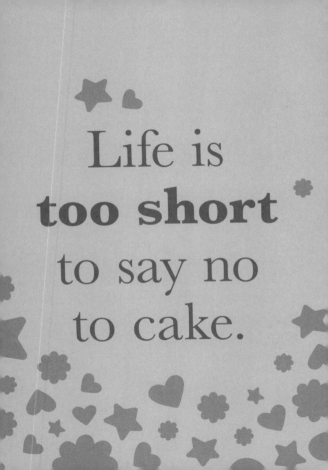

Life is
too short
to say no
to cake.

Chocolate Balls
(*Chokladbollar*)

Makes about 15 (1½-inch) balls

Chokladbollar are simple treats that are fun to make with children. They require no baking, so if you are searching for a quick chocolate fix, these are for you. If you like, roll the balls in a coating, such as cocoa powder, coconut, or chopped toasted almonds. For an adult version, substitute 1 tablespoon rum and 1 tablespoon espresso for the 2 tablespoons espresso.

½ cup granulated sugar

7 tablespoons (3½ ounces) unsalted butter, softened

¼ cup unsweetened cocoa powder

2 tablespoons brewed espresso coffee

1 teaspoon vanilla extract

1¼ cups old-fashioned oats

Pinch of sea salt

Toppings:

Cocoa powder, cocoa nibs, pearl sugar, coconut, finely chopped toasted almonds

1. In the bowl of an electric mixer fitted with the paddle attachment, cream the sugar and butter until light and fluffy, about 3 minutes. Add the cocoa powder, espresso, and vanilla and mix until smooth. Mix in the oats and salt. Transfer to a bowl, cover with plastic wrap, and refrigerate for 30 minutes.

2. Roll the mixture into 1½-inch balls. If using a topping, roll in the topping to coat. Place the balls on a parchment-lined baking tray and repeat with the remaining chocolate dough.

3. Refrigerate the balls for at least 30 minutes before serving. The balls may be refrigerated in an airtight container for up to 1 week.

There is always time for tea and cake.

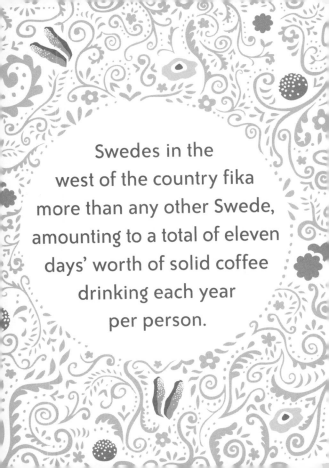

Swedes in the
west of the country fika
more than any other Swede,
amounting to a total of eleven
days' worth of solid coffee
drinking each year
per person.

Fruit

Blueberry Soup
(Blåbärssoppa)

Serves 4 to 6

In Sweden, bilberries (wild European blueberries) and cultivated blueberries are used interchangeably in this healthy soup. It's a refreshing and simple summer dessert, with a dollop of Greek-style yogurt or whipped cream or a drizzle of heavy cream. During the height of the berry season, extra berries are often frozen so they can be enjoyed year round. In the winter, this soup is served slightly warm, for a healthy taste of summer past.

3 cups fresh or defrosted frozen blueberries

2 cups water

¼ cup granulated sugar

⅛ teaspoon ground cinnamon

1 tablespoon fresh lemon juice

2 teaspoons cornstarch

1. Combine the blueberries, water, sugar, and cinnamon in a medium saucepan. Bring to a boil over medium-high heat, stirring to dissolve the sugar. Decrease the heat to medium-low and simmer until the berries begin to break down, about 10 minutes.

2. Whisk the lemon juice and cornstarch in a small bowl until smooth. Add to the berries and simmer until slightly thickened, about 5 minutes.

3. Cool slightly and serve warm, or cover and refrigerate and serve chilled.

Strawberry Rhubarb Compote
(Jordgubbs-och Rabarberkompott)

Serves 6

Rhubarb is the first harbinger of spring in Scandinavia, and strawberries herald the peak of summer. Luckily, early strawberries are grown in greenhouses, so the dream team of strawberries and rhubarb can be enjoyed in this compote. This characteristically simple dessert is a comforting favorite, served with a drizzle of whipping cream.

1½ pounds rhubarb, ends trimmed, cut into
    ½-inch slices

1 pound strawberries, hulled and halved
    (quartered if large)

⅔ cup granulated sugar

2 tablespoons fresh lemon juice

½ teaspoon vanilla extract

Heavy cream, for garnish

1. Combine the rhubarb, strawberries, and sugar
   in a large saucepan and cook over medium heat,
   stirring until the sugar dissolves. Decrease the
   heat to medium-low, partially cover the pot, and
   simmer until the strawberries release their juices
   and the rhubarb is soft, 25 to 30 minutes. Stir in
   the lemon juice and vanilla.

2. Remove from the heat and cool to room
   temperature. Serve at room temperature or
   chilled with a drizzle of heavy cream.

Sandwiches & Flatbreads

Cured Salmon (Gravlax) on Crispbread
with Honey Mustard & Dill

Makes 2 pounds cured salmon

Gravlax literally means "salmon in a grave or hole." During the Middle Ages, fishermen would salt salmon and let it ferment by burying it in a hole above the high-tide line. Nowadays, salmon is coated in a brine of salt and sugar and banished to the refrigerator to cure. Fresh or dried herbs, peppercorns, citrus, or spirits are often added to the simple brine for extra flavor. This recipe includes dill, fennel, and coriander. The cured salmon can be stored in the refrigerator for up to 4 days.

Salmon:

1 (2-pound) center-cut, skin-on salmon fillet,
  pin bones removed

1 large bunch fresh dill sprigs

½ cup chopped fennel fronds

½ cup kosher salt

¼ cup granulated sugar

1 teaspoon coriander seeds, toasted and
  coarsely ground

1 teaspoon coarsely ground black pepper

1. To prepare the salmon, rinse the salmon and pat
dry with paper towels.

2. Place a piece of plastic wrap about 3 times the
width of the salmon on a work surface. Place half
of the dill and half of the fennel in the center of
the plastic.

3. Combine the salt, sugar, coriander, and pepper
in a bowl. Rub the skin side of the fish with some
of the salt mixture. Arrange the salmon, skin side
down over the top of the dill and fennel. Spread

the remaining salt mixture over the top of the salmon, gently rubbing it into the flesh. Scatter the remaining dill and fennel fronds over the salmon.

4. Wrap the plastic tightly around the salmon and place skin side down in a baking dish. Place a heavy pan or a tray on the fish to weigh it down. Refrigerate for 2 to 3 days, flipping the fish every 12 hours or so.

Mustard:

¼ cup canola oil

¼ cup Dijon mustard

2 tablespoons cider vinegar

2 tablespoons honey

2 teaspoons finely chopped dill fronds

¼ teaspoon sea salt

¼ teaspoon freshly ground black pepper

5. To make the mustard, whisk all the ingredients in a small bowl until emulsified. Cover with plastic and refrigerate until use.

6. To serve, remove the fish from the refrigerator and remove and discard the plastic wrap. Pour off any collected juices and wipe off the excess brine and dill from the salmon with paper towels.

7. Slice the salmon on the diagonal from one corner of the fillet toward the center.

For Serving

Rye or multigrain crispbread, such as Wasa

Unsalted butter

Fresh dill fronds

Lemon slices

8. To serve, fold a slice of gravlax on a buttered crispbread. Drizzle with 1 to 2 teaspoons of the honey mustard. Garnish with the dill fronds and a lemon slice.

Open-Face Shrimp Sandwich
with Egg, Crème Fraîche & Lemon
(*Raksmörgås*)

Makes 4 open-face sandwiches

Open-face sandwiches (*smörgås*) are little pieces of art, thoughtfully layered with fresh, seasonal, and colorful ingredients. Shrimp *smörgås* are usually served on white bread, not dark rye bread, which can overpower the shrimp's sweet and delicate flavor. Tiny fjord shrimp are typically used on these sandwiches in Scandinavia, but bay shrimp are an easy substitute.

4 center-cut slices Italian or French bread loaf, ½-inch thick

Lightly salted European-style butter, softened

8 butter lettuce leaves

2 hard-cooked eggs, cooled and sliced ¼ inch thick

Sea salt and freshly ground black pepper

¾ pound (125/175 count) cooked bay shrimp

⅓ cup crème fraîche (or whole milk Greek yogurt)

4 dill sprigs

1 lemon, quartered lengthwise

1. Spread each bread slice with the butter and cover with two lettuce leaves. Arrange a layer of sliced eggs over the lettuce and lightly season with salt and pepper.

2. Arrange the shrimp over the eggs, piled in neat rows. Spoon a heaping tablespoon of crème fraîche in the centers of the shrimp and top with the dill sprigs. Garnish with black pepper and serve with the lemon wedges.

Swedish Sandwich Cake
with Smoked Salmon, Cucumber & Radish (*Smörgåstårta*)

Serves 8

Smörgåstårta is a popular sandwich cake that includes salad and seafood layered between bread, bound together with an "icing" of whipped cream cheese or a blend of cream cheese and sour cream. There is no single way to make this cake; favorite fillings include hard-cooked egg, smoked salmon, baby shrimp, cucumber, and avocado. The cakes may be simple or extravagant—so it's up to you to be as creative as you like. This savory cake is best eaten immediately or within 2 hours of preparing.

1 large round country-style bread, such as levain, about 9 inches in diameter

4 cups whipped cream cheese, divided

4 tablespoons finely sliced chives, divided

Sea salt and freshly ground black pepper

1 English cucumber, thinly sliced

6 to 8 large radishes, thinly sliced

6 ounces thinly sliced smoked salmon

2 tablespoons finely chopped red onion

2 tablespoons fresh dill fronds

½ cup (loosely packed) Italian parsley leaves

2 teaspoons finely grated lemon zest

1 tablespoon capers, drained and rinsed

1 large hard-cooked egg, cooled and sliced ¼ inch thick

1. Trim off the domed top of the bread and reserve for another use. Cut off the crust on the bottom and around the edges of the bread so that the loaf is round and flat topped with straight sides and is completely crustless. Slice the bread horizontally into three equal layers, about ½ inch thick each.

2. Smear 1 to 2 tablespoons cream cheese in the center of a serving plate. Place one bread layer on the plate over the cream cheese to prevent it from sliding. Spread about ⅓ cup cream cheese over the top of the bread. Sprinkle 2 tablespoons of chives over the cream cheese and lightly season with salt and black pepper. Arrange two layers of cucumber and radish slices in concentric circles, slightly overlapping, over the cake. (You can use any remaining slices to decorate the top of the cake.)

3. Spread about ⅓ cup cream cheese on a second bread slice. Place the bread, cream cheese side down, over the bottom layer. Brush the top of the bread with about ⅓ cup cream cheese and lightly season with salt and black pepper. Layer the salmon over the cream cheese. Scatter the onions and dill sprigs evenly over the salmon.

4. Spread about ⅓ cup cream cheese over the remaining bread slice and place, cream cheese side down, over the salmon. Refrigerate the cake for 1 hour to allow it to set.

5. When you are ready, spread the remaining cream cheese evenly over the top and sides of the sandwich cake. Gently press the parsley leaves onto the sides of the cake. Sprinkle the lemon zest over the top of the cake and arrange the capers around the perimeter. Arrange the egg slices in a concentric pattern in the center of the cake. Add any remaining cucumber and radish slices in concentric patterns around the egg, if desired.

6. Sprinkle the remaining 2 tablespoons chives over the top of the cake and garnish with black pepper. Serve immediately or refrigerate for up to 2 hours before serving.

Worry often gives a small thing a great shadow.

—Swedish proverb

When the going gets tough, the tough take a coffee break.

—Stephen Hawking

Metric
Conversions &
Equivalents

Metric Conversion Formulas

To Convert	**Multiply**
Ounces to grams	Ounces by 28.35
Pounds to kilograms	Pounds by .454
Teaspoons to milliliters	Teaspoons by 4.93
Tablespoons to milliliters	Tablespoons by 14.79
Fluid ounces to milliliters	Fluid ounces by 29.57
Cups to milliliters	Cups by 236.59
Cups to liters	Cups by .236
Pints to liters	Pints by .473
Quarts to liters	Quarts by .946
Gallons to liters	Gallons by 3.785
Inches to centimeters	Inches by 2.54

Approximate Metric Equivalents

Volume

¼ teaspoon	1 milliliter
½ teaspoon	2.5 milliliters
¾ teaspoon	4 milliliters
1 teaspoon	5 milliliters
1¼ teaspoon	6 milliliters
1½ teaspoon	7.5 milliliters
1¾ teaspoon	8.5 milliliters
2 teaspoons	10 milliliters
1 tablespoon (½ fluid ounce)	15 milliliters
2 tablespoons (1 fluid ounce)	30 milliliters
¼ cup	60 milliliters
⅓ cup	80 milliliters

½ cup (4 fluid ounces)	120 milliliters
⅔ cup	160 milliliters
¾ cup	180 milliliters
1 cup (8 fluid ounces)	240 milliliters
1¼ cups	300 milliliters
1½ cups (12 fluid ounces)	360 milliliters
1⅔ cups	400 milliliters
2 cups (1 pint)	460 milliliters
3 cups	700 milliliters
4 cups (1 quart)	0.95 liter
1 quart plus ¼ cup	1 liter
4 quarts (1 gallon)	3.8 liters

Weight

¼ ounce	7 grams
½ ounce	14 grams
¾ ounce	21 grams
1 ounce	28 grams
1¼ ounces	35 grams
1½ ounces	42.5 grams
1⅔ ounces	45 grams
2 ounces	57 grams
3 ounces	85 grams
4 ounces (¼ pound)	113 grams
5 ounces	142 grams
6 ounces	170 grams
7 ounces	198 grams
8 ounces (½ pound)	227 grams
16 ounces (1 pound)	454 grams
35.25 ounces (2.2 pounds)	1 kilogram

Length

⅛ inch	3 millimeters
¼ inch	6 millimeters
½ inch	1¼ centimeters
1 inch	2½ centimeters
2 inches	5 centimeters
2½ inches	6 centimeters
4 inches	10 centimeters
5 inches	13 centimeters
6 inches	15¼ centimeters
12 inches (1 foot)	30 centimeters

Oven Temperatures

To convert Fahrenheit to Celsius, subtract 32 from Fahrenheit measurement, multiply the result by 5, then divide by 9.

__Description__	__F°__	__C°__	__British Gas Mark__
Very cool	200°	95°	0
Very cool	225°	110°	¼
Very cool	250°	120°	½
Cool	275°	135°	1
Cool	300°	150°	2
Warm	325°	165°	3
Moderate	350°	175°	4
Moderately hot	375°	190°	5
Fairly hot	400°	200°	6
Hot	425°	220°	7
Very hot	450°	230°	8
Very hot	475°	245°	9

Common Ingredients & Their Approximate Equivalents

1 cup uncooked white rice = 185 grams

1 cup all-purpose flour = 140 grams

1 stick butter (4 ounces • ½ cup • 8 tablespoons)
= 110 grams

1 cup butter (8 ounces • 2 sticks • 16 tablespoons)
= 220 grams

1 cup brown sugar, firmly packed = 225 grams

1 cup granulated sugar = 200 grams

Information compiled from a variety of sources,

including *Recipes into Type* by Joan Whitman and Dolores Simon (Newton, MA: Biscuit Books, 1993); *The New Food Lover's Companion* by Sharon Tyler Herbst (Hauppauge, NY: Barron's, 2013); and *Rosemary Brown's Big Kitchen Instruction Book* (Kansas City, MO: Andrews McMeel, 1998).

A cup of coffee
shared with a friend is
happiness tasted and
time well spent.

The Little Book of Fika

Andrews McMeel Publishing
a division of Andrews McMeel Universal
1130 Walnut Street, Kansas City, Missouri 64106

www.andrewsmcmeel.com

24 25 26 27 28 SHO 14 13 12 11 10

ISBN: 978-1-4494-8984-7

Library of Congress Control Number: 2017953308

Editor: Jean Z. Lucas
Designer: Sierra Stanton
Production Editor: Maureen Sullivan
Production Manager: Carol Coe

Attention: Schools and Businesses

Andrews McMeel books are available at quantity discounts
with bulk purchase for educational, business, or sales
promotional use. For information, please e-mail the
Andrews McMeel Publishing Special Sales Department:
sales@amuniversal.com.